poetry
under
the
sheets

Ruel Fordyce

If beauty is pain,

Let me get lost in it

If you're my salvation,

I want to earn it

If love is all I have to give,

Then let me give it

CONTENTS

Childhood Dreams

Twas the night;
and the sky lit
with many stars
seemed magical.

In the midst of silence,
my cerebrum
is thinking aloud
about love.

I'd heard it
the day before;
the song
that continuously
replayed in my mind.

Ruel Fordyce

I was nine years;

too young,

but in time

love I will find.

The melody

and the lyrics

that entered

and crowded

my soul.

Que, sera, sera,

whatever will be,

will be,

the future

is not ours to see,

que, sera, sera.

What does a young boy know about love?

poetry under the sheets

Unable to fathom

the depths

of such

expressions.

She was

the prettiest girl

I had ever seen.

Long black hair,

brown eyes

and her skin

was smooth

and fair.

Under the lights

her beauty shone

like a halo,

and there I was

thinking about love.

Ruel Fordyce

What does a young boy know about love?

Whatever it meant,
it felt like love
at first sight.

The wind chimed
and thinking
to myself,
I wanted her
to be mine.

Her father
was a pastor,
and oh
how I wanted
to tell her
that I loved her.

poetry under the sheets

But no, not me!
He was a strict man
with his daughter.

Premature at best
but it's what I felt.

She was the only one.

It did not matter
if the room was full
of other girls.

She was the one.

She had to be the one;
stuck in my mind
and I won't let go;
she was my
childhood dream.

Ruel Fordyce

What does a young boy know about love?

As she sang,
my eyes focused
on her beautiful
bolero jacket.
It covered
the top of her
Cinderella dress.

She had
the nicest shoes
I'd ever seen,
but maybe I was
blinded by love,
or for the least
my version of it.

poetry under the sheets

Just a kid
with no stress
or responsibilities
and enjoying life
for all it's worth.

It felt like
it was my time
but no it wasn't,
yet in time
love I'd find.

But I'll have to wait
and there went
my little Kate.

She was all that
I want her to be,
she was perfect
just for me.

Ruel Fordyce

But for the moment,

it wasn't the reality.

But I prayed

that one day

it will be

the possibility,

that she'll

wait for me.

She was all

I dreamt

her to be,

she was

my childhood

dream.

Idle Hands

The devil

always finds work

for idle hands to do.

The plight

of a curious teenager;

it was a Sunday afternoon.

Anxiety is the

unsuspecting company

that awaits

the leave of absence,

as they proceed

to a function

only for grown-ups.

Ruel Fordyce

Nothing good arises

out of a situation

with a pair

of idle hands,

for this is what happens

when you leave

a teenager

at home alone.

Spending long hours

on the phone

and it was the least,

of their worries.

Oh be careful little eyes

what you see,

it will corrupt

your mind and

skew your perception

the conscience said.

poetry under the sheets

But another voice spoke
and yet curiosity
must be satisfied.
Those idle hands
as a teenager,
did things no parent
could ever approve.

Those days
of video cassettes,
and the video shop
was just around
the corner.

Updated, X-rated
and filthy for the mind.
It always felt wrong,
especially when
an adult sold it
to a kid.

Ruel Fordyce

Those things were not,

for impressionable minds.

It's an irony

that those things,

were never found

in white but

non-transparent

black bags,

that made you feel

as guilty as sin.

Curiosity kills the cat,

when a teenager

with raging emotions

is curious to know.

But how else will he know,

if no one tells him?

poetry under the sheets

Sex is not,

the kind

of conversation

a kid usually has

with his parents.

Home alone or wait!

There was

three of us;

Me, the TV

and that

video cassette.

Oh be careful

little eyes

what you see,

the voice spoke.

Ruel Fordyce

But the reality

of rated images

across the TV

with no one around

but me,

increases

the excitement

even more.

But is was so

easy to ignore

the thought

of being caught and

my eyes wore fixed

to the screen,

while the temperature

rose disproportionately

in that infamous region.

poetry under the sheets

It just reacted,

it wasn't thinking

especially as the brain

was numb.

It stood erect,

tall, bold

and proud.

He had arisen

from the dead.

It was the strangest

and yet the most

exciting feeling

I've ever had.

Ruel Fordyce

Home alone with

those idle hands,

but every minute

my eyes were

constantly looking

at the door.

It's one

of those moments,

where one

must always be

on the lookout,

for the unexpected visitor

especially if its

those two,

who gave birth

to you.

poetry under the sheets

Ten minutes
of inflated ecstasy
and boom
a volcanic eruption
of hot lava spews
all over the place.

If it could've spoken,
it probably would tell
of how violated it felt
and how it was robbed
of its innocence.

It's the very thing
that no one
wants to get caught
doing,
for it will be
an embarrassment.

Ruel Fordyce

Play, fast forward

and don't forget

to rewind,

better yet,

make sure it does

not get stuck

in the VCR.

This isn't a subject

a male teenager

wants to discuss

with his parents.

But what is a teenager to do?

There's nothing wrong

with experimenting,

but it was

the easiest way to learn

anything about sex.

poetry under the sheets

Maybe I had

the wrong interpretation

but it was always

the perception,

that this was

what love was.

But who knows

what love is?

If there's anyone

with wisdom

surely its

the best

kept

secret.

Ruel Fordyce

But these eyes

beheld total strangers,

with many fingers

and many toes

exposed

with no clothes.

And it was

a sure way

to skew

any definition of love

but as a teenager,

why would I even care?

And as the scenes rolled,

it revealed the same narrative

over and over again

but with different actors.

poetry under the sheets

For the least

it shouldn't be

that awfully boring,

but after the first scene

it's easy to see

that there's no creativity,

or spontaneity

and it was

quite predictable,

yet my idle hands

wanted to know.

No one spoke

of these things

but there I was,

molding my mind

thinking that all women

wanted the same thing.

Ruel Fordyce

Maybe this was love

or maybe it wasn't,

maybe this was how

a woman

wanted

to be treated.

But what was done

in secret

always comes

to light,

when there's a trail

of evidence.

There's no place

to hide

or time to lie,

because the truth

always wins.

Welcome to Adulthood

Time waits on no one

and it doesn't

give options

or chances

to choose,

while the next moment

lurks and creeps

into existence.

A mind that has

already been

molded by

the digital world.

Ruel Fordyce

I'm no longer a child,

but a man

should be fully aware

that he must

take responsibility

for all of his actions.

Yet the expectancy

of wise decisions,

still finds me

making mistakes.

Successfully matriculated,

well-educated,

so smart choices

should be the norm

and never an option.

poetry under the sheets

The first day,

in the world of work,

unveils the reality

of things

one normally

does not see.

Sitting in the lunch room

and just wanting

to have lunch,

I nearly choked,

when the damsel entered.

She proceeds

to the refrigerator

and bending over,

there was barely more

than a string,

that covered

her essential parts.

Ruel Fordyce

As we made

eye contact

she spoke,

good day!

welcome to the

CREW's Inn.

Maybe she forgot

to look in the mirror.

She wore a skirt

that was transparent

as the daylight,

and short

as one's memory.

Who was this?

And why was she dressed that way?

poetry under the sheets

But my sinister mind

couldn't help

but think

that this was

an easy target.

Imagination wasn't a fairytale.

I could see

with my naked eye

and was nearly caught,

looking to find

the land that flowed

with milk and honey.

After all, I'm but just a man.

My eyes were graced

with the wonder

of sweet nothingness.

Ruel Fordyce

She was voluptuous

from top to bottom

and the thought

of enjoying her,

awakened the Mr.

that was dead.

The boats that were

docked near by

and her wear

told a different story.

I was there to work

but she was a supervisor

on vacation.

She was protecting

her interest

as her yacht

was docked outside.

poetry under the sheets

A single mother

with a daughter

and her wear

gave the impression

of a woman

in dire need

of experiencing

my magic stick.

The apple

doesn't fall

too far

from the tree

as her daughter

entered through

the door

some moments

after.

Ruel Fordyce

But it was just a taste

of the real world,

where people

hide their problems

behind covers

and smoke screens.

Striking a conversation

with the daughter

who was the younger

version of her mother;

she was in every way

a freak.

She was plain about it

as she spoke.

We are all adults

with no need for disguise.

poetry under the sheets

We are free to be
however we want to be,
no hiding how we feel
but I wasn't prepared
for what came next.

Without warning
thrust into a situation
and No!
this wasn't a movie
it was the real thing.

She portrayed herself
like a faithful concubine,
devouring every part
of my anatomy
as the scenes unfold.

Ruel Fordyce

But it was

never the plan

as we find

a room as dark

as the midnight cover

on work,

robbing each other

of our breath

and she was

firmly positioned

on the magic stick.

She takes

the enchanted ride;

up and down

and we both

enjoy ourselves

on the Ferris wheel

of fantasy.

poetry under the sheets

We play a game

of Russian Roulette;

load the bullet

and spin the cylinder

and hope

it never triggers

or we both

get fired

if anyone knows.

This is the real world

where people pretend

but she never had

any social values.

That was

of little concern,

for her mother

was wealthy

and spoiled her rotten.

Ruel Fordyce

But that wasn't

my story;

at least I knew

what was right

and yet it was a struggle

to not become

a part of the backward norm

that society

had grown into.

All work and no play

is what they say

makes Jack a dull boy

but growing older

should make one wiser

but no one knows

what awaits us

in the future.

poetry under the sheets

I never wanted

to live my life in folly

and not understand

what it really means

to be a man,

but damn it

my kryptonite

was always a woman.

But my perception

of who she was

took its root

and found its premise

in promiscuity.

But can you blame me?

It was the norm

and she wanted it

just like I did

and I aint no punk.

Ruel Fordyce

But one thing

lead to another

and soon enough

I was lost for numbers;

greater than

my ten toes

and fingers,

full of ego

and to some

their hero;

the accumulation

of numerous escapades

and within dense circles

lay the achievements

of many accolades.

It was is every way

the norm

and she was the definition

of what was revealed.

poetry under the sheets

It's funny

hearing them speak

of men

and describing them

as worthless dogs

But if I can milk the cow

without pay for it,

what do you expect?

Clearly you are not

the one I'll ever

want to take home.

It's not me but you

who needs a reality check,

maybe in retrospect

you should examine

your priorities.

Ruel Fordyce

The Things We Do For Love

It's said that love

has many eyes

but if love ever had eyes

it's probably blind.

The crazy things

we do for love,

with our eyes wide open

and no! It's not,

the other person's fault.

as we've convinced

ourselves to believe.

poetry under the sheets

It's a man world;

ruminating in the moment

of James Brown

and sipping on a cold drink

and gazing at the damsel

across the bar

as both our eyes meet.

Walking over and

the usual introduction

in midst of her friend

and an offer on the table

to buy the next round

of drinks.

The waiter approaches

and sex on the beach

is the order of the day

and a little later

I had her phone number.

Ruel Fordyce

Noticeably absent

after agreeing to meet

the boys

for a football match

earlier that night,

I chose to forego

the game,

only to find myself

the first night

in the confines

of her space,

to bury the length

of my soul

inside of her

and she was

a total stranger.

poetry under the sheets

Every time

I entered,

it felt like

the first time.

But it was a lie!

The door was opened

many times before.

I must be crazy,

to even engage

in an unholy war

without protection.

She was gifted

and as far

as I can remember,

she was spicier

than a ginger,

with needs that only

a man could fill.

Ruel Fordyce

I was stupid
and couldn't see
that it was always
a bad agreement
from the begining.

Whoever said
that all
that starts well,
ends well
certainly told a lie.

Some things
are destined
for bad endings.

Some people
are too toxic
for your health.

poetry under the sheets

But controlled

by that region

between her thighs,

a man's magic stick

is powerless.

What is this?

Maybe my mind

is playing games

but I can't

muster the courage

to leave.

She mutters

the word love,

but I aint having

any of it

for this isn't love.

Ruel Fordyce

Love is hard

and should never

be that easy.

She wants

to be committed

to one man

but she's not committed

to time,

to release

her past hurts.

Her story carries

the same narrative

over and over again.

She was a woman

of little self-worth

and my presence

didn't make it better for her.

poetry under the sheets

She was always

in need of being

in the company

of someone.

She was uncomfortable

with being alone

and could never accept

the thought

of self-introspection.

Seeking affection

in all the wrong ways

and giving of herself

but never receiving

the equivalent.

Ruel Fordyce

It always felt

like someone

stole something

from her;

A paranoia

that I am

getting "sick" of.

I saw you watch her!

So should I close my eyes?

The streets became

the stomping ground,

for her boisterous voice.

In plain sight

and even if I tried

to look away,

I'm accused

of mirroring

her past hurts.

poetry under the sheets

But she was

a crazy b*tch

with many shades

of emotions;

from love to hate

to being unsure

about our flings

and back to love

and then eventually hate.

She was the classic definition,

of a schizophrenic.

But I'm worse than her

because I continue to stay

in the same situation,

with the option

to leave but I don't.

Ruel Fordyce

There are many

fishes in the sea,

but the power

of that region

between her thighs,

ensured that I was

caught in her trap.

She had more shades

than one could find

on a colour wheel.

From ranting

like a mad woman

in broad daylight

to begging at night

for forgiveness.

poetry under the sheets

What in seven hells,

did I see in this woman?

But that region

between her thighs

clouds my vision

and makes me do

stupid things.

I've been whipped

and we sink

to a new low.

It couldn't get worse

I keep telling myself

and thinking;

How stupid can I be?

Ruel Fordyce

But now I'm engaged

but should disengage,

to release myself

from the trap

I entered into

with eyes wide open.

No two people

should knot their lives,

if they live like enemies.

But it was a disguise

and those intense sessions

misrepresented

the terms

of our agreement.

poetry under the sheets

But the crazy things

we do for love,

makes us

abnormal creatures

of bad habits.

There's no explaining

the stupidity

and believing

that false realities,

will correct themselves

to make us happy.

Such thinking

is for the mentally unfit

and the ultimate definition

of insanity.

Ruel Fordyce

Yet, it's the common trap

and I must admit

I did fall into it.

At some point,

one must admit,

that the pursuit of love

makes us do

crazy stupid things.

Square Pegs and Round Holes

Listen well!

If you're lucky

to escape from a bullet,

run like hell

and never look back.

But the stupidity

of my decisions,

is no better than

a dog that returns

to its vomit.

Ruel Fordyce

It is very important

to pay close attention

to the history

of a relationship.

If it didn't flourish

in times past,

what guarantee

is there

that it will

work in the present?

The knot

was almost tied

but stupidity

keeps returning

to that region

between her thighs.

poetry under the sheets

It couldn't be

that good,

but damn it!

it was!

It was the

awaited breakup

and just when I thought

I was free,

there's always

a way

to make a mess

of life.

We weren't

on speaking terms,

yet the familiar itch

reminds us of the fire

that continually burns.

Ruel Fordyce

It was never
destined to work,
but blind to the fact
finds us in the act
once again.

I keep telling myself,
that this
is just temporary
until I find
another chick.

It's mutually agreed,
we are both here
for shared benefits.

poetry under the sheets

It's a dangerous

and slippery slope

that leads me

to act like,

a law abiding citizen

in the day

and creeping

like a thief

in the night,

to steal the last

of her inheritance

and ruin her future.

No clue

of what to expect,

except,

for being

in the moment.

Ruel Fordyce

Trying to fit

a square peg

in a round hole,

is the definition

of crazy

and yet it's

the common trap.

Wasn't it

just a moment ago,

when she seemed

to be happy?

It leads me

to question many things

and now my sanity

is under threat.

poetry under the sheets

But out of nowhere

she transforms

into fifty shades

of crazy

and it hits me

like a ton of bricks,

when she tries

to move

to the next level

but it's not

my desire.

I've misunderstood,

but it was never

my thought

to mend

a broken chain.

Ruel Fordyce

It was always

an agreement

for shared benefits,

yet experience teaches

how foolish

one could be.

To believe

in what was said

and not realize

that the heart wants

what it wants

is the classic trap.

And the cycle

starts all over again.

poetry under the sheets

From love,

to being unsure

of what

this thing was

and back to hate.

It has to be over now.

Yet, the stupidity

of such thinking

raises its ugly head.

But when

you've been hit

by a bullet,

you must admit,

that you're

in need of help.

Ruel Fordyce

All that's done

in darkness,

will find its way

to bite one

in the butt.

I've had enough

and the b*tch

must go.

But then

several weeks

roll away

and thinking

I was free

a call comes to say

there's a bun

in the oven.

poetry under the sheets

It seems justified

for being stupid

in entering a war

without a shield.

Thinking to myself,

I could deny it

with no visible signs,

but in my heart

I know it could be true.

And who told me

to question

her sincerity?

The very thought of it,

sparks another moment

of untold insanity.

Ruel Fordyce

She wants

the world to know,

of the crimes

committed against her,

yet somehow

I convince her

to prevent the smell

from escaping.

An act of desperation

leads to the betrayal

of the unborn.

She turns off the heat

and the bun stops rising;

it never finishes

and we both

will never know

the outcome.

The Conversation

When stupidity

becomes a pattern,

it's time to yield

to the stranger

that knocks

at your door;

her name

is called wisdom.

It's the father-son talk,

where age brings reason

and wisdom comes

in grey hairs.

Ruel Fordyce

The folly of youth

exposes immaturity

and the errors

of one's ways

is blind

to the perpetrator.

It's the long

and dreaded conversation

about the portrait

of his past

and I can't muster

the courage

to get up,

but out of respect

I stay to hear him say,

you've got to do better

with your life.

poetry under the sheets

Life is never easy

but when

I took it for granted,

it punished me

with the reminder

of my mistakes.

We all make mistakes

but we must learn

from them.

Sowing one's seed

like wild oats,

will lead to nowhere,

except to ruin your life.

Barely looking into his face

because of shame,

as past reflections

resurrect from the grave.

Ruel Fordyce

A life

that was headed

to ruin,

until someone

decided to speak

common sense

to the one

who lacked it.

A timely intervention,

that would save my life.

No one is perfect

but never

stop trying,

to be the best

that you can be.

poetry under the sheets

Real love

sees the best

in others

even when

they cannot see

it in themselves.

No one

can judge you

except for God.

A bad start

is not the end

of your story.

Start over,

rewrite the scenes,

but end with purpose.

Ruel Fordyce

There's nothing better

than good advice;

no price tags,

freely given

and received.

The more

the mind reflects

on wisdom,

the easier it is to see

that it's always right.

Longing for that change

but couldn't find,

the key that opens

the future.

poetry under the sheets

Yet, there's always

an opportunity,

to erase the mistakes,

sharpen a new way

and write a new story

on the blank pages of life,

for there's a new beginning,

where the best

is saved for the ending.

A new chapter begins.

The New Chapter

If I've learnt
anything from life,
it's to live everyday
like it's the last.

Love is precious
and no one knows
when it may be gone.

But a new day dawns
in the horizon,
and love always shines
from the rising
till the set of sun.

poetry under the sheets

Sitting one morning

In the coffee shop

I was captivated

by her beauty.

Her radiance shone,

like a beacon of light.

The beauty

of her simplicity

came with

no accessories.

She was

the breath of fresh air

that I longed for.

Ruel Fordyce

Shuffling across

the room

and introducing myself

with pleasantries.

She seemed different

to the type of women,

I am attracted to.

As if she had

a magnifying glass

she saw

right through me.

She speaks,

I'm not here

for small talk,

if you cant

engage my mind

keep moving.

poetry under the sheets

And who does she

think she is?

Aint no woman

talk to me

like that before.

She'd better

take her head

out of the clouds

and experience

a real man.

But she was

that woman

who knew her worth

and no empty words

will fool her.

Ruel Fordyce

She's been saving "it"

for the person,

who understands

that she's not

a "one night stand".

She speaks,

I'm not going

to give you my number

unless I'm sure

that I can be

comfortable around you.

Who are you?

What do you do?

What ambitions do you have?

What the hell is this?

poetry under the sheets

Who does she think she is?

Asking me
all these questions
as if she were
a lawyer
and I her
hostile witness
on the witness stand,
waiting to be
interrogated.

I looked her
straight in the eye
and she was as frank
as frank can be.

I'd better think
of something fast
or this will be the end.

Ruel Fordyce

But I'll have

to agree to disagree

to see her

at the coffee shop

to engage her

in conversation.

Usually I would

keep moving

if I couldn't taste her

within a reasonable time

and yet something

about her

intrigued me.

And it took

three months,

before she exchanged

her number.

poetry under the sheets

But time is like

a casino dealer

with a deck of cards

that shuffles and

deals the hand.

True love

will never hide

or fear,

when a bad hand

is exposed to the core.

I'll be brave,

placing them face up

and marching forward,

knowing that time

always brings

opportunities.

Ruel Fordyce

For there is

nothing to fear,

if truth

is always

the main dish

on the plate.

A tainted past

against a clean slate;

how could I ever compare?

Am I worthy of her love?

There's no touching

or hugging,

its just conversation

and I must work

to win her over.

poetry under the sheets

To know what

she does,

what she's interesting in

and not what's

between her legs,

this was always going

to be a challenge.

She has a big heart

for seconds chances

but she was warned

to not be foolish

and give away

her prized possession.

And it may seem unfair

that someone like me

whose been around,

should ever find love

with this woman.

Ruel Fordyce

Shocking but true

and out of the blue,

after many months

she agrees

to see where it goes,

but no one knows

if it's a wise decision,

but only time can tell.

I grasp all opportunities

with both hands,

never to let go,

as I seek to

re-write my story.

It's never a bad idea

to remember the past,

if it helps define

a better future.

poetry under the sheets

If I ever
mess this up,
I'm cursed
to a life of singleness.

It's not her but me,
who must prove
that he's worthy,
of her love,
time,
and her life,
never to add
to the strife.

And all the things
I was after,
appeared to be
meaningless
as I turned
a new chapter.

Colours of Love

No one knows

what love is

in its entirety,

but if I had

to describe it,

the definition of love

would be like

a powerful nexus,

draped in

a kaleidoscope

of colours.

Without love,

life ceases to exist.

poetry under the sheets

And feels like yesterday

but her love

is like a rainbow

and deep within

that intricate soul,

I behold,

her compelling beauty.

Sometimes love

makes me

want to do

the unthinkable.

It's that type of love

that is filled

with adventure

and the spontaneity

of our raw emotions.

This is the love that craves.

Ruel Fordyce

On the canvas of life,

the hue of passion

is splashed

in copious measures.

But when love embraces,

I hold onto her

and never to let go.

And love,

is sometimes expressed

on a chilly night

under the sheets,

and reveals itself

through scenes.

A mixture of cold

and warm drafts

that sparks

a hurricane moment.

poetry under the sheets

It's that type of love

that caresses

every contour

of the body,

and when love

touches me

my body quivers.

Her love comforts

like the soft glow

of twilight

and she is

the reflection

of complete serenity.

Love moves

through her fingers

and is filled

with sweet sentiment.

Ruel Fordyce

Love is

the amalgamation

of many colours.

Who has seen its full spectrum?

But love is

always present,

when obscurity blinds

the pathway

to happiness.

Love is sentimental

and quite seductive;

a prerequisite

that ultimately leads

to the land of ecstasy.

poetry under the sheets

Love is that nexus

that enters my soul

and even my sleep,

and like air beneath

a bird's wings,

it keeps lifting me higher

to heights unimagined.

Love has its own sound

and I dance to it,

at the sunrise

of early morn.

Love is the heartbeat

of life

for without it

I'll surely die

and when I've failed,

love shows me

how to try.

Ruel Fordyce

If I let her

she takes me

to that place

far away in wander,

and quietly in the midst

I see the colours

and I ponder.

Love

- perseveres through all circumstances

- cares when no one else would

- provides peace in troubled times

- revels in humility

- makes amends for all wrongs

- sees the good in others

- fills a need before its own

- smiles, though situations are grim

- forgets all wrongs

- knows no evil

- always speaks the truth

poetry under the sheets

- defends when no one else can
- believes where hope fades
- envisions a brighter future
- preserves the good times

Ruminating

in the moment,

I could hear

that love harmonizing

among the boisterous

cyclones of wind,

and even

in the deafening silence

her voice is as distinct,

like water that flows

from a fountain.

In the midst of uncertainty,

love often emerges

like an oasis

from a desert.

it matters not

if she's surrounded,

for she makes ripples

in the widest and

deepest of waters.

Love freely

cuts through

the infinity

of space.

and doesn't

need anyone's

approval.

Love is that gift

that exists

giving to all,

without hesitation

and without limits.

poetry under the sheets

With so many attributes

it's a wonder

that no one

has seen

the entire spectrum

of colours,

and I'm still amazed

yet never fazed

or dazed

by the colours

of love.

Ruel Fordyce

The Day I Prayed For

Love has met me

standing in the aisle

waiting for the one

who takes

my breath away.

She was

more radiant

than when I first

saw her

at the coffee shop.

poetry under the sheets

The element

of surprise,

lead to the

unbelievable day

that fulfilled the wish

of all dreams.

Behind the veil

that covered

her face;

she was

the embodiment

of my greatest dream.

She was worth it

and good things

come to those

who wait.

Ruel Fordyce

The moment

commences

in music and

the congregation

of eyes

were fixed

to the highlight

of the moment,

as the luckiest man

beheld

the most precious

gem in the world.

Love comes

in second chances

and second chances

do have good endings.

poetry under the sheets

Expressions of tears

with all fears

cast away;

it was the moment

previously captured

in anticipation.

Indeed it was the day I hoped for.

Standing there

in her presence

was a heart

that yearned

to be loved.

How could I ever let her go?

The celebration

of a new life together.

Ruel Fordyce

What God joins,

let no man

put asunder;

through sickness

and health

till death do us part.

Looking through

the lens of love

it felt unreal,

but I was

in the presence

of reality.

The knot was tied

this time

and must be

cherished forever.

poetry under the sheets

Two hearts

joined together

as one;

for love

no longer speaks

as a child

but as

a grown man.

Former mistakes

are now forsaken

to the past,

and love leads

to the encounter

that journeys

unto the future.

Ruel Fordyce

Here and now

and always

I promise

to love faithfully.

She was all I ever needed.

Make the moment

last forever,

by never forgetting

to recapture the scenes.

A display of love

that reveals

the purest

of moments

that is forever

shared together.

poetry under the sheets

As deep night

shades fall,

the joy of two

connected halves

makes the scene

of love complete.

Two lives

forever changed

with a new

set of responsibilities

that finds

its premise in love.

It was

the defining moment,

it was

everything I dreamt of.

Definition of a Woman

When no one

understands her,

she speaks

with a strong voice.

But to find that voice is awfully hard.

She speaks

not only by words

but also by actions,

she speaks

clearly and concisely.

poetry under the sheets

She's never a slave

to the wishes

of fantasy.

She knows

her worth,

for she's more

than the

reciprocator

of life.

Beautifully designed

to love,

she smoothens

the coarseness

of life.

She was, is

and always will be

the greatest role model.

Ruel Fordyce

She is as delicate
as the perfect rose,
no one should ever
pluck her petals.

She beams
like the glitter
of gold;
she's filled
with confidence
unsurpassed.

Don't be fooled,
she's more than
what's revealed
on the surface.

She's like fine wine
that gets better with time.

poetry under the sheets

Seek to understand her,

listen as she speaks

from the heart,

she is not

as complicated

as we were

led to believe.

Patience is her virtue

and when her voice

is misunderstood,

she speaks in monotone

and the theme is love.

She is

the demarcation

of class

and finesse

is her wear.

Ruel Fordyce

She walks

and her charisma

exudes.

She understands

thrift,

yet at times

she craves

to be spoiled.

Never be afraid

to give her

what she wants.

She is the heartbeat

and the cornerstone

of the family

for she is its nucleus.

poetry under the sheets

She forgoes

her wants

and ensures

her loved ones

make their

greatest stride,

for she is indeed

a woman of pride.

She smiles

through the pain

of circumstances.

She is the testament

of true strength.

Ruel Fordyce

She forgives

when she's hurt

and her love

transcends

beyond its worth.

She speaks through natural beauty.

She's bold

and confident

and simple

and she knows

who she is.

She is

the definition

of a woman

with the fragrance

of uniqueness.

poetry under the sheets

She is

never concerned

about living

to the expectations

of others

for she is perfect

in her own way.

She is not afraid

to surrender

her body, soul

and her deepest will

to the man

deserving of it.

She is a woman

who is worthy

of honour;

she is deserving

of respect.

Ruel Fordyce

She is,

a personal organizer

who rarely forgets.

She cries,

she laughs,

she loves,

when life seems grim.

She was and still is

in every way the definition

of a woman,

for her beauty

always lied within.

And this is the woman,

I vowed to spend my life with,

for she is the woman,

I've fell in love with

over and over again.

Romantic Chivalry

If chivalry was dead,

she has certainly

awoken it.

She is the woman

that I'll open

the door for.

She is the woman

I'll pull the chair for

and allow to sit

before I do.

Ruel Fordyce

I'm not
the type of guy
to prepare meals
but for her I will.

I'll gladly
do the chores
even if my muscles
are sore
from a long day
of work,
for she is
deserving of it.

And we sit
around the table
ready and able
to devour
what has been
prepared.

poetry under the sheets

An exotic drink,

festive rice,

vege lasagna,

barbecue chicken,

black beans

and steamed broccoli

with carrots.

A delightful carrot cake

with Haagen Dazs,

Belgium chocolates,

and Jello

with glazed fruits

awaits for desert.

She's never to lift

a finger,

for tonight is the night

where she'll

be spoiled.

Ruel Fordyce

Gazing into her eyes,

I love to hear

her speak

and moving

my chair

closer to hers,

I whisper

the sweet fragrance

of romantic words.

And as our lips

meet together

I am addicted,

to the feeling of it

pressing against mine.

We are perfect

for each other;

a match

made in heaven.

poetry under the sheets

As we lay

on the sofa

cuddling each other,

the warmth

of our bodies

ignites a special heat,

as my fingers

run through her hair

and then to her back.

Nibbling on her ears,

while I continue

to create

poetry in motion.

And it's ok to be kinky

just for a bit,

while modeling

in underwear that resembles

an elephant's trunk.

Ruel Fordyce

Tonight it's all about her,
but the mood must be right.

Lights dimmed
with lighted
scented candles
and roses petals scattered
all over the floor
and a bottle of wine
in a chiller filled with ice.

But chivalry
has no limits
for she has
awoken it.

poetry under the sheets

As the music plays,

I slowly dance

towards and on her

as she would

do for me.

And tonight

she's allowed

to treat me as if

I were her slave.

I allow her to place

the handcuffs,

as I submit

to her fantasy.

And she blows

my mind

in ways that

I never imagined.

Ruel Fordyce

Romantic chivalry

is not dead;

it's in every way

alive.

Wine, whipped cream

and peaches

around her navel,

and a tongue

that weaves the splendor

of sweet ecstasy.

Caressing her feet,

soothing her fingers

and massaging

her back

as the mood

is being set.

poetry under the sheets

It takes time

to romance her

but patience

will be rewarded.

If the beauty

of romancing her is pain,

let me get lost in it.

If she is my salvation,

I want to earn it.

If love is all I have to give,

then let me give it.

But what started

on the sofa,

transcends to another place,

where all wishes

are granted.

She Moves Me

My experiences

have taught me

that when

the winds

of love blow,

I should dance

for it is

the essence of life.

Beauty always lies

in the eyes

of the beholder.

poetry under the sheets

She was smooth,

modest

and sexiness

oozed

from her soul.

And I'm proud

to say she is mine;

the one and only

I'll give my love to.

We find ourselves

in a carousel

of emotions,

and she amazes me

every time

with the adventure

of freedom.

Ruel Fordyce

Her creativity
is priceless
and she captivates
my mind.

She is the bearer
of humour with
a refreshing view
of reality.

And our love
is that rare epic
that connects two
phenomenal minds.

She is the beginning,
middle
and
end
of my sentences.

poetry under the sheets

She draws me

into her

and stimulating

my mind

in ways

I've never

imagined.

Like seconds in a minute,

she is as precious

as time.

To see her face

every morning

is like the novelty

of an unopened gift.

Ruel Fordyce

Her inner beauty

is like the iron

that comes

from an ore;

oh how

it attracts me

even more.

She is not easily predictable.

I knew it then

and even now

that I am in love.

She was and is

the highest prize.

She is my gold medal,

attained on

the highest level.

poetry under the sheets

Love emotionally

connects us together,

but love appears

to be simple

yet it's not,

for it takes

a lot of effort.

This love

feels too good

to be true,

but I've always

trusted my heart

to lead the way.

And now I know

that I was created

to love.

Ruel Fordyce

Love takes us

to the realm

of the unknown

where two hearts

are joined

together as one,

forever belonging

to each other.

And she still moves me.

A sensual woman

who causes my mind

to race like speed

is to a fast car.

My heart still races

only for her.

poetry under the sheets

And I still want

to do things to her

in unforeseen places.

Drip, drip, drip,

the fragrance of lavender

infused along

the contour

of the body

and a pair of hands

that invokes

the spell of ecstasy.

I slowly caress

her breasts

and her nipples

stand at attention

enroute to an

enchanted climax.

Ruel Fordyce

And the very thought

of her

moves me

in ways,

that nature

could never

compare.

Like the wind,

passion blows

through our minds,

bodies,

souls

and

spirit's sphere.

And she moves me

like nectar

moves with bees.

poetry under the sheets

And she moves me
like the treble
and bass clef notes
on a music sheet.

And her love is
always perfecting
that special
master piece
within me,
to find tone,
balance
and harmony.

She makes my soul
to rest at ease.

She moves me
through the science
of love.

Ruel Fordyce

And my soul

yearns for her

through

kinetic motion.

Like the sun

in its full glory

and in all its rays,

her love

penetrates me

like heat waves.

She fills my life

with sensuality

and intense passion.

She moves me

in ways that makes

it impossible

to resist her.

poetry under the sheets

I explore

every part

of her body

as if she were

a treasure chest.

And the chill

of ice

running down

the middle

and a tongue

that slowly travels

to the valley

of the tittle.

And I discover

that the plains

have been trimmed

exposing the surface

of a virgin land.

Ruel Fordyce

I meditate

for as long as I can,

for this is the valley

where dreams

are heightened

and the atmosphere

is heavenly.

I wash my face

in the pond

that lies

between

the oasis.

I drink

and drink until

I am drunk

with ecstasy.

poetry under the sheets

And I immerse

my soul

into calm waters

and make

huge ripples

that sound

like a symphony

and the wave notes

follow in crescendo

across minor

and major chords.

Skip a beat

but it's not over.

In quiet will

the sound staccato's

and I'm jamming still.

Ruel Fordyce

Depress the lever

into full throttle

and penetrate

right through

the middle

for X marks

the g spot.

And we make music,

as the sounds

of high notes

come crashing through

the final bars,

into the blissful

flight of victory.

This was

the monumental ride

of pure delight.

poetry under the sheets

And she moves me

in ways

that I couldn't imagine

life without her.

She is the joy

of my life,

and there's no other

and yet my soul

still fodders.

Even when

our hairs are grey

I can always say.

She still moves me

with knuckle knees.

She still moves me

to see a new day.

Ruel Fordyce

As it was in the beginning

so shall the end be,

through life's up's

and down's

she still moves me,

in every way

to rock her world.

About the Author

Delta Function a.k.a Ruel Fordyce grew up in the beautiful Island of Trinidad and Tobago. He is a graduate of the University of Greenwich and enjoys writing short books that help people to achieve their best in life. Ruel is married and lives with his wife in Trinidad and Tobago. You can follow Ruel on Instagram at **Delta Function.**

Made in the USA
San Bernardino, CA
30 October 2017